# 101 CATACLYSMS

## FOR THE LOVE OF CATS

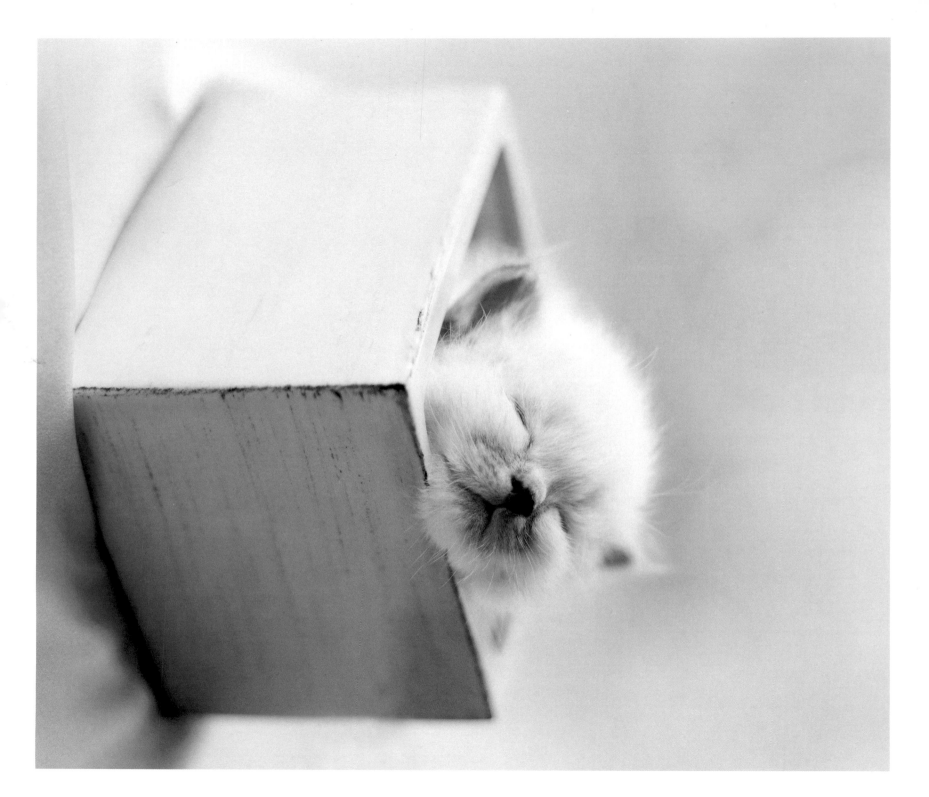

# 101 CATACLYSMS

## FOR THE LOVE OF CATS

RACHAEL HALE

Bulfinch Press

New York • Boston

FOR ALL THE CATS
WE LOVE AND CHERISH –

ESPECIALLY EDMUND!

The uninitiated of the human species believe a cat is a cat. Yes, every cat is alike in that they are independent creatures, who come home to eat and sleep before wandering off to do what ever business a cat must do. But it is obvious the unversed have never met a cat like Pat.

Pat is a strapping, black and white domestic short hair — or "moggy," as we New Zealanders call them — who lives at my local veterinary clinic. Most days you will find him curled up on top of the computer in the clinic, or waiting on the receptionist's swivel chair for someone to give him a whirl. But Pat's real passion is travel, and the sign on the clinic door warns visiting pet owners to thoroughly check their vehicles for the adventurous cat before they drive away.

Soon after I had captured a classic "cool cat" Pat pose for this book, news came of his latest trip — a five-kilometer ride atop a car, the driver oblivious to her passenger, gleefully roof-surfing through busy city streets. I'm certain Pat has been blessed with 18 lives.

Pat is no ordinary feline, but then none of the 101 cats photographed for this book could ever be classified as ordinary.

In my endeavors I have been enlightened, and thoroughly captivated, by clever, nimble, impish, loveable cats — and every one different from the last. While to the untrained eye most cats look alike but for the shape of their eyes or the rich hues of their fur, every cat I have met is a unique individual.

I quickly ascertained there were different ways to work with different breeds. The Persians were funny and floppy, but some of them could also be highly strung. The Asian cats were often naughty but brimming with character; the Burmese the most mischievous; the Russian Blues shy and unsure of the big outside world; the "moggies" all sweet-natured.

Capturing cats on film was a much more challenging task than photographing dogs. Most of the time, dogs will sit where you ask them to, but you can never pick up a cat, place him on the spot and expect him to stay there.

He will always stand up, affronted, and walk straight back to where you fetched him from. I now entice cats with my Hansel-and-Gretel technique – laying down morsels of food in a trail to where I want them to go. You must possess a vast amount of patience to overcome "feline fickleness." When you finally capture that character and attitude on film, it's worth the hours spent. The trick is to get to know the cats and let them feel they trust you. I would spend hours letting them take their time to approach me, schmooze against my legs and eventually lay claim to my lap. Just one cat put me in my place with a swift swipe of the paw – my only wound after years of photographing animals. After he drew blood, he seemed satisfied that he was in control of the situation, and we got on famously.

Some of the cats displayed incredible tolerance themselves. Nikon, a "moggy" I have known for many years, was a model of poise and patience. He was chosen to pose with his friend Nigel because of his special gentle nature and even with a mouse on top of his head, he simply stared deep and calmly into the camera lens.

Every photograph was shot in the cat's own environment – in a studio, it would have taken them days to settle. I do my utmost to avoid ever putting animals under stress, or forcing them to do anything against their will, so it was important to choose cats who were comfortable under the spotlight. Some were initially nervous about the big lights and strange camera I would bring along – an imposing 4 x 5 inch large-format camera like an old-fashioned box with the black cape over the back. But, as naturally inquisitive creatures, I would give them time to investigate the equipment.

I have learned so much about my own triumvirate of cats – the roguish Himalayan Persian Edmund, and my designer "moggies" Gianni and Versace – through this mission, and now look at them with a totally new respect.

I have used official terminology wherever possible, but please be aware that names, breeds, and colors of cats vary slightly from region to region.

I definitely believe in the quote "Dogs believe they are human. Cats believe they are God." Cats are so fiercely independent and free spirited, but thank goodness, they still feel the need to humour, protect and make a fuss of us humans every now and again.    RACHAEL HALE

It's one for the money, two for the show,

three to get ready, now go, cat go!

CARL PERKINS, "BLUE SUEDE SHOES"

1. HOBBIE  2. MINDY  3. TYSON  4. KC  DOMESTIC SHORTHAIR AND LONGHAIR

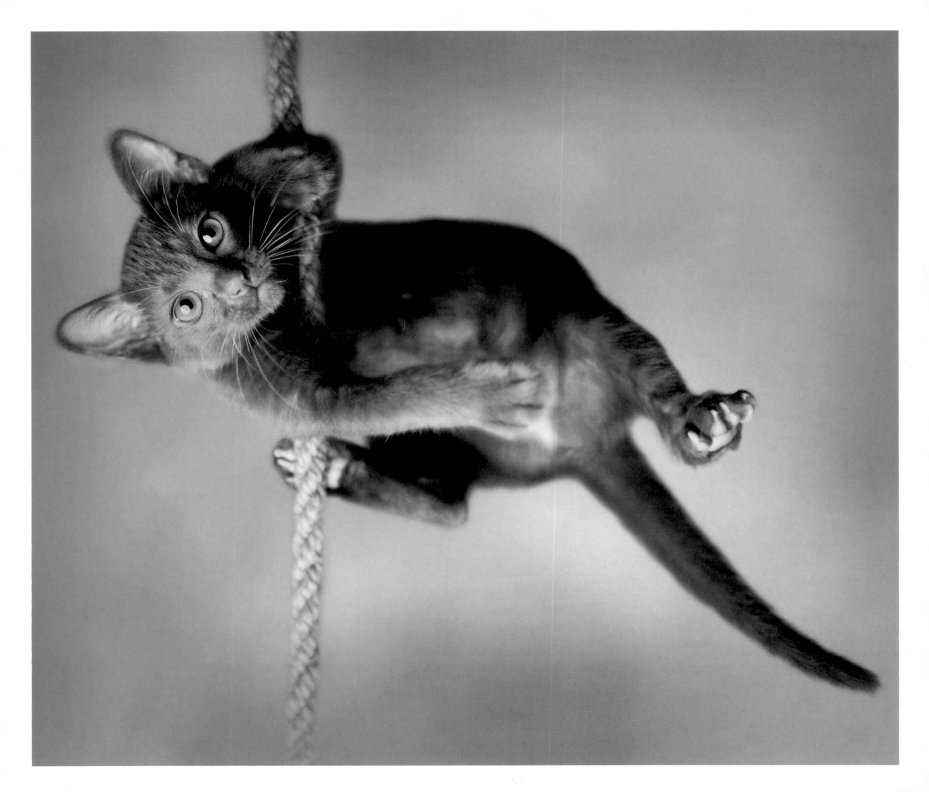

The smallest feline is a masterpiece.

LEONARDO DA VINCI

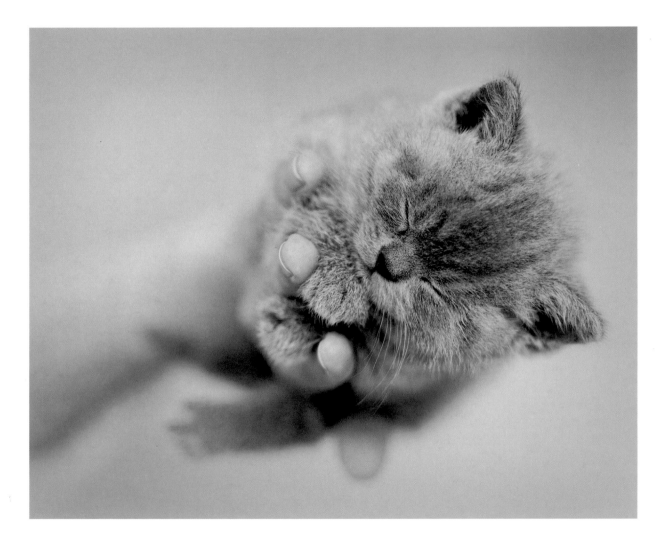

7. MAXIMUS BRITISH SHORTHAIR ▼

8. PENELOPE HIGHLAND VARIANT ▼

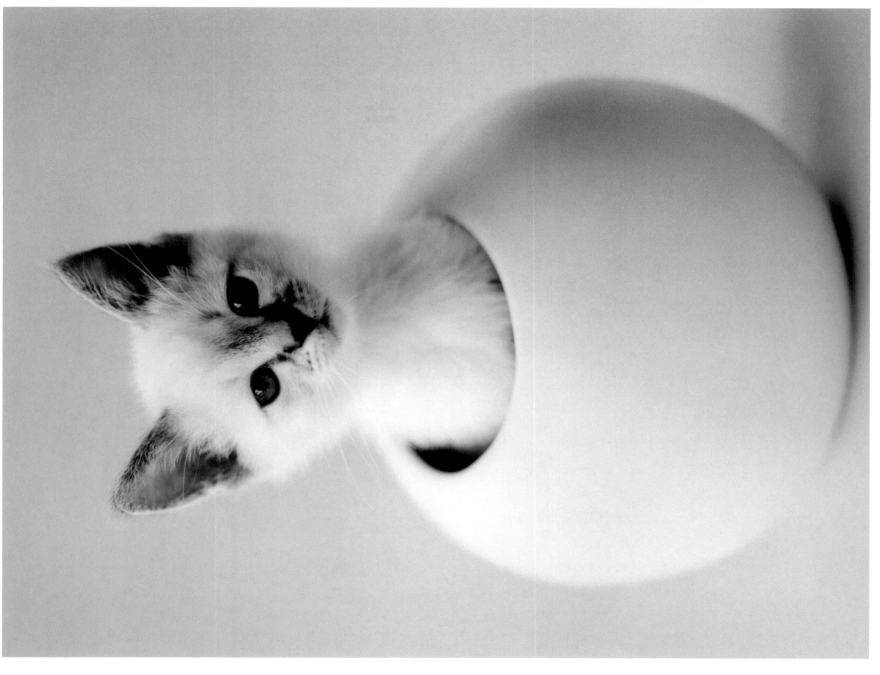

10. WIZARD OF OZ TEMPLE CAT ▲

11 & 12. SEBASTIAN AND AZZURRO ASIAN SHORTHAIR ▼

13 & 14. SUNRISE & DAWN BROWN MARBLED BENGAL ▼

Cats are connoisseurs of comfort.

**JAMES HERRIOT**

15. YABBA DABBA DOO BLUE POINT BRITISH SHORTHAIR ▼

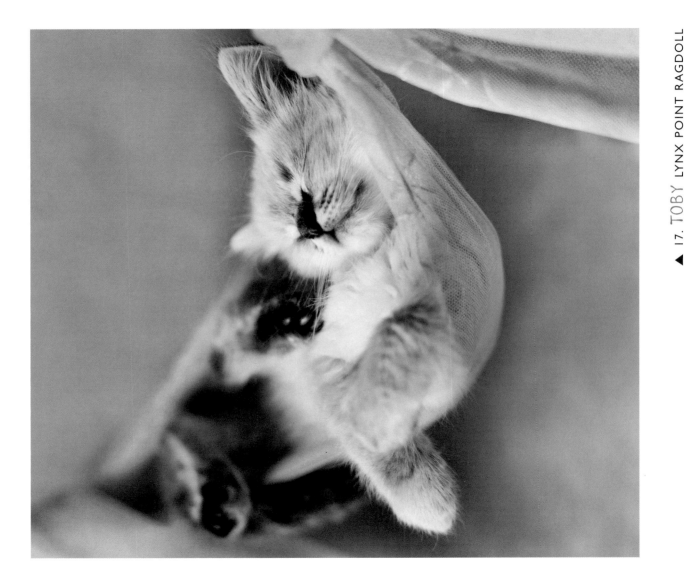

▲ 17. TOBY LYNX POINT RAGDOLL

GIANNI & VERSACE

18 & 19. DOMESTIC LONGHAIR

Cats are rather delicate creatures

and they are subject to a good many

ailments, but I never heard of one

who suffered from insomnia.

JOSEPH WOOD KRUTCH

24 & 25 GUINESS & FATBOY DOMESTIC SHORTHAIR ▼

In ancient times cats were worshipped as gods,

they have never forgotten this.

ANONYMOUS

# RAMSEY

▼ 27. CYMRIC

29. TRINITY RUSSIAN BLUE CROSS ▲

To bathe a cat takes

brute force, perseverance,

courage of conviction — and a cat.

The last ingredient is usually

hardest to come by.

**STEPHEN BAKER**

▼ 31. COUGAR DOMESTIC TABBY

# EDMUND

32. HIMALAYAN PERSIAN ▼

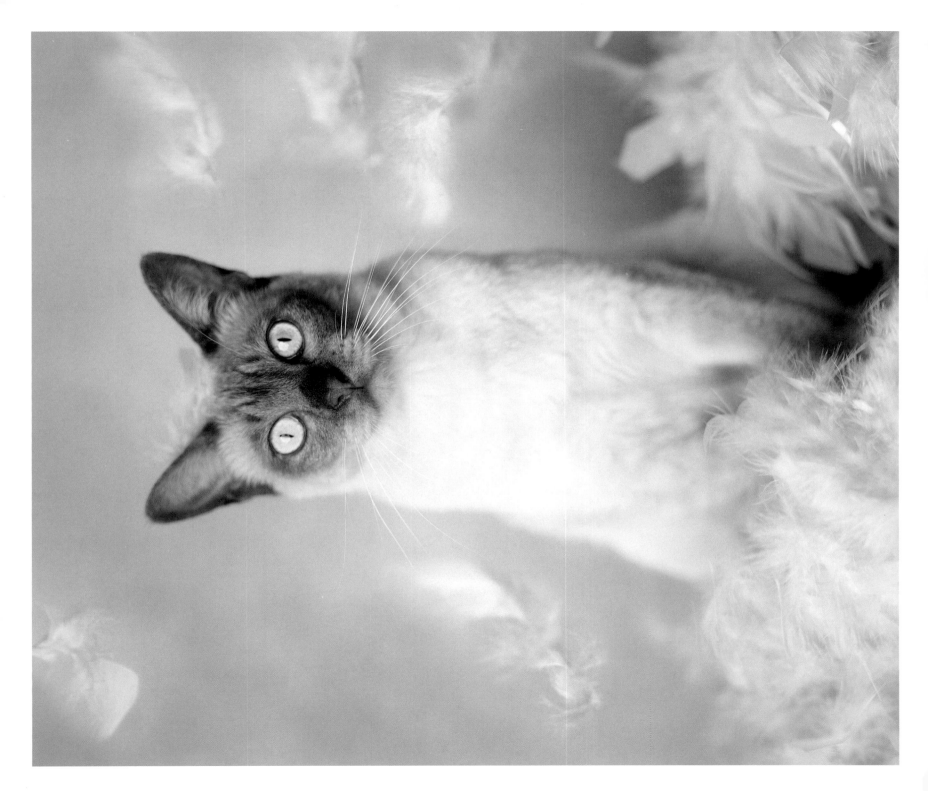

We looked!

Then we saw him step on the mat!

We looked!

And we saw him!

The Cat in the Hat!

DR. SEUSS

# MERLIN

40. SCOTTISH FOLD

The more people I meet

the more I like my cat.

ANONYMOUS

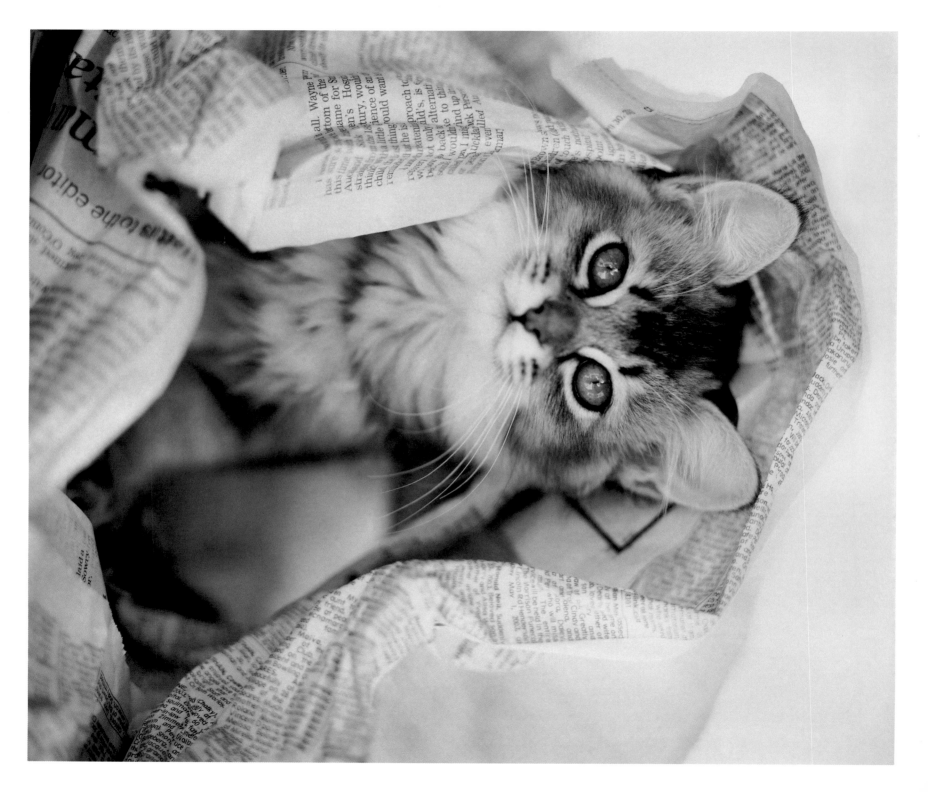

VENEZIA

▼ 41. BROWN TABBY TIFFANIE

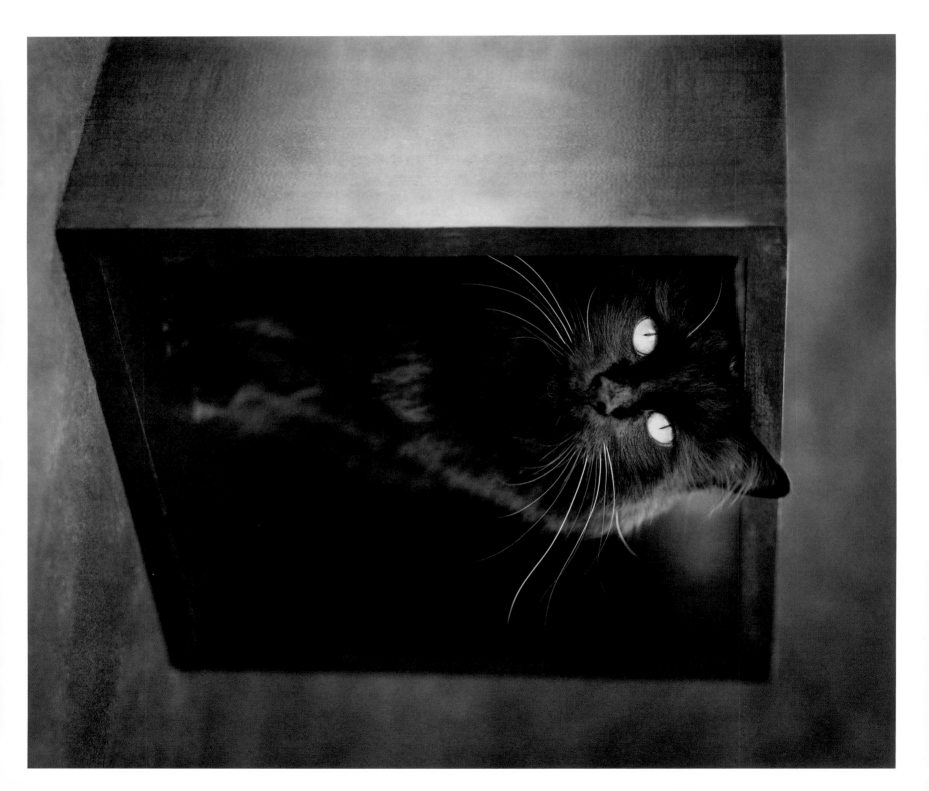

CHLOE

▼ 43. DOMESTIC LONGHAIR

# TEDDY

44. RED TABBY EXOTIC ▼

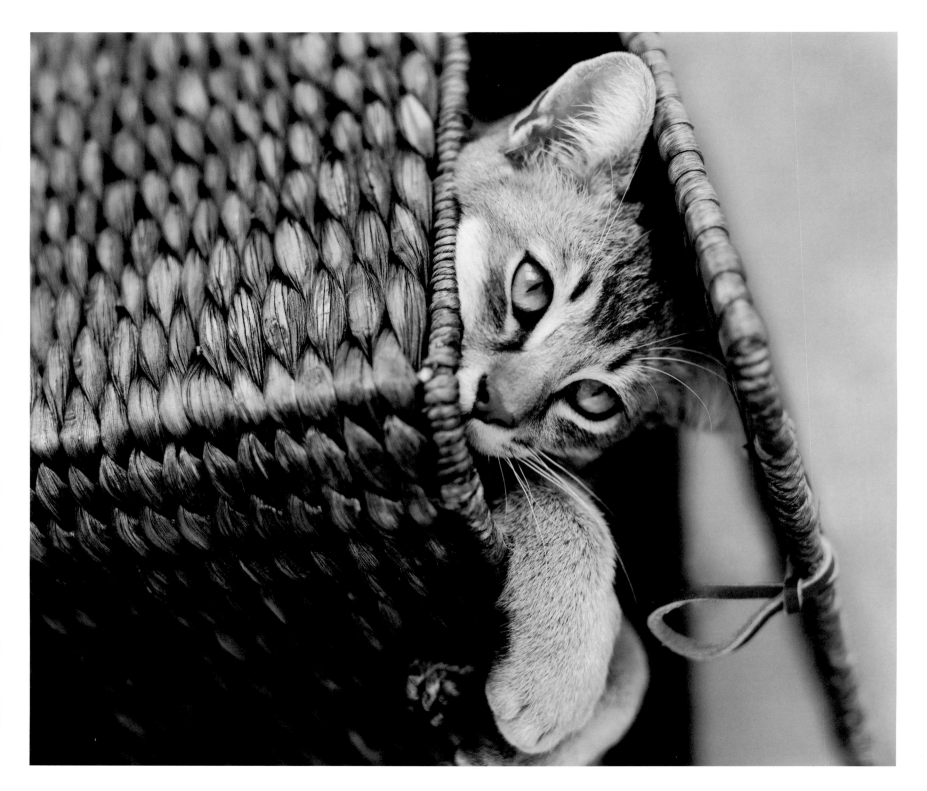

TOSCANO

▼ 45. ASIAN SHORTHAIR

A cat has nine lives.

For three he plays,

for three he strays,

and for the last three he stays.

**ENGLISH PROVERB**

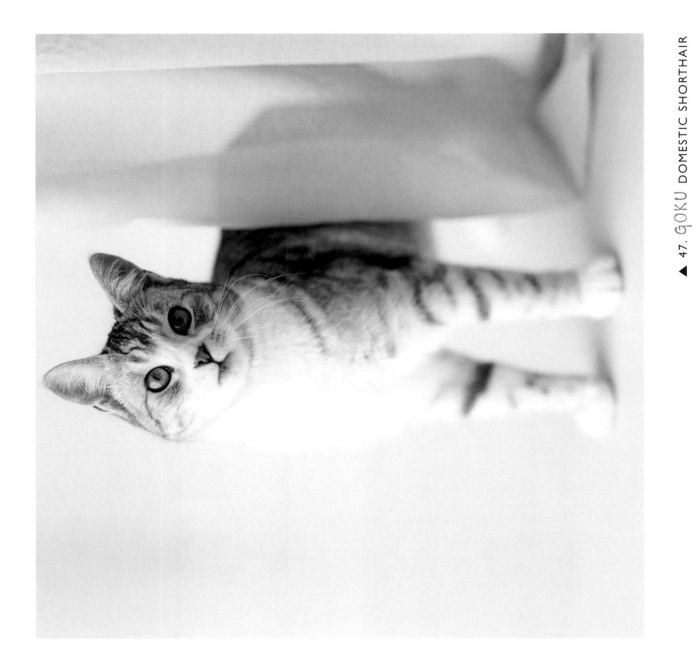

▲ 47. GOKU DOMESTIC SHORTHAIR

WINNIE

48. DOMESTIC TABBY ▼

BIG BOY PUSS

▼ 51. ISLE OF MAN

When she walked...she stretched

out long and thin like

a little tiger, and held her head

high to look over the grass as if

she were treading the jungle.

**SARAH ORNE JEWETT**

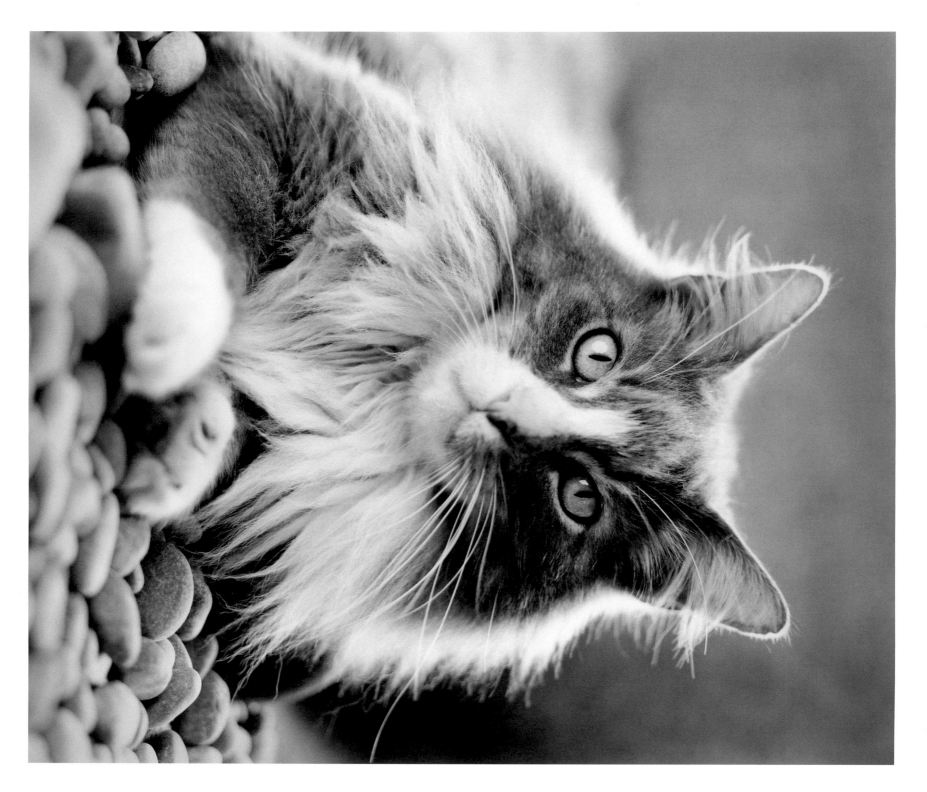

# CROSBY

▼ 55. CYMRIC

After dark all cats are leopards.

AMERICAN PROVERB

56. ERROL SEAL BURMESE ▼

# TIN TIN

▼ 59. RUDDY ABYSSINIAN

If man could be crossed with a

cat it would improve man, but

it would deteriorate the cat.

**MARK TWAIN**

▼ 60. *CASTELLO* SNOW MARBLED BENGAL

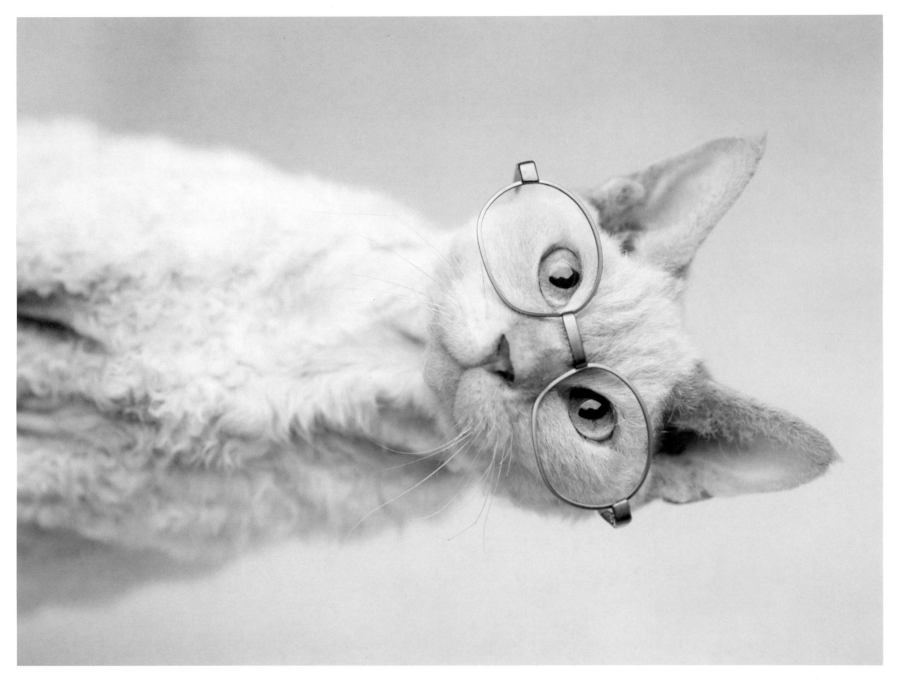

▲ KANGO DEVON REX. 61

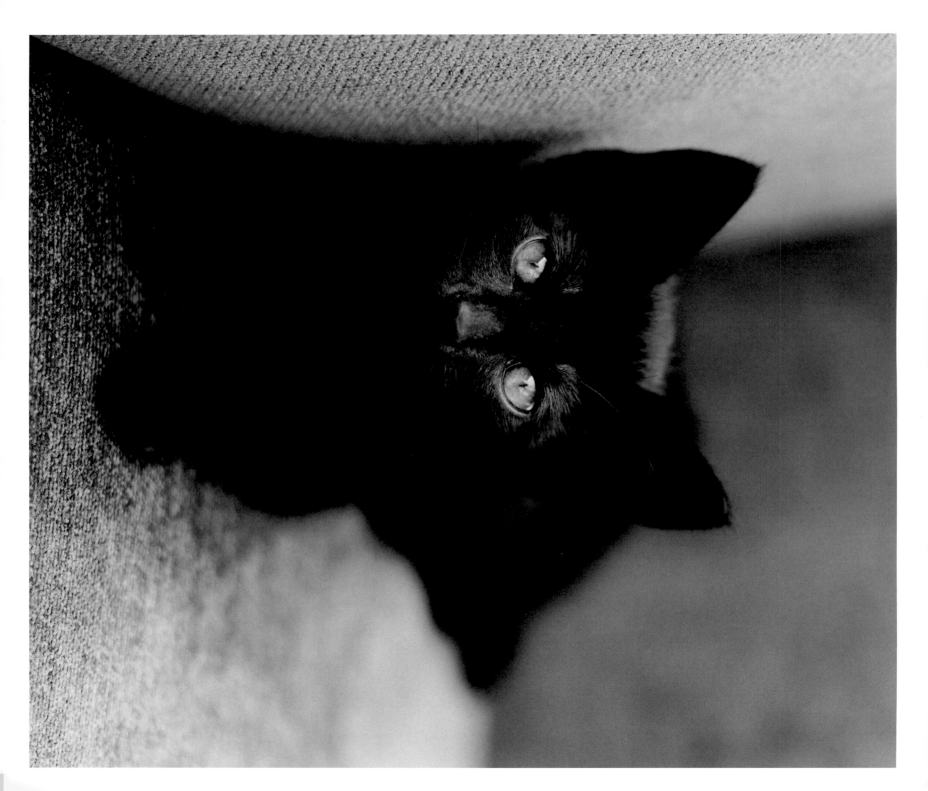

A kitten is chiefly remarkable

for rushing about like mad

at nothing whatsoever, and

generally stopping before it gets there.

AGNES REPPLIER

▼ 63. SCRUFFY DOMESTIC SHORTHAIR

Pussycat, pussycat, you're so thrilling

and I'm so willing, to care for you....

Pussycat, pussycat, I love you!

TOM JONES, "WHAT'S NEW PUSSYCAT?"

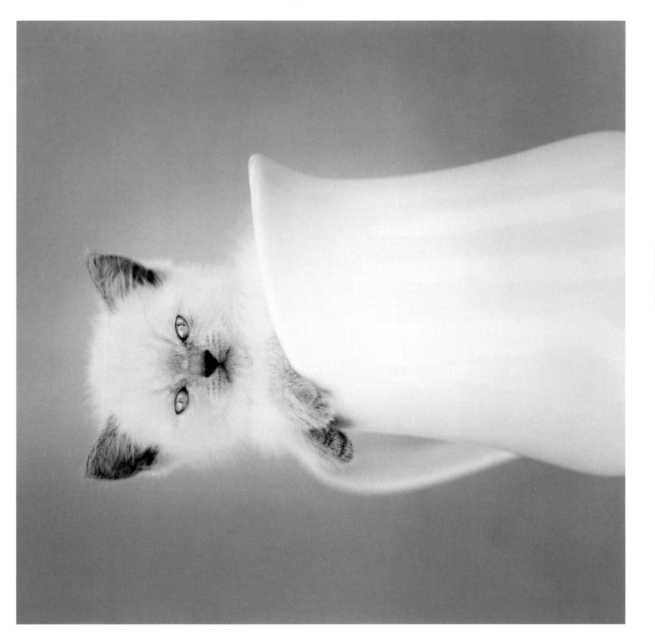

▲ 72. CASPER BLUE POINT BRITISH SHORTHAIR

It is with the approach

of winter that cats...

wear their richest fur and

assume an air of sumptuous

and delightful opulence.

**PIERRE LOTI**

73. NEVADA SHADED SILVER PERSIAN ▼

77. OSCAR KORAT ▼

Dogs believe they are human.

Cats believe they are God.

ANONYMOUS

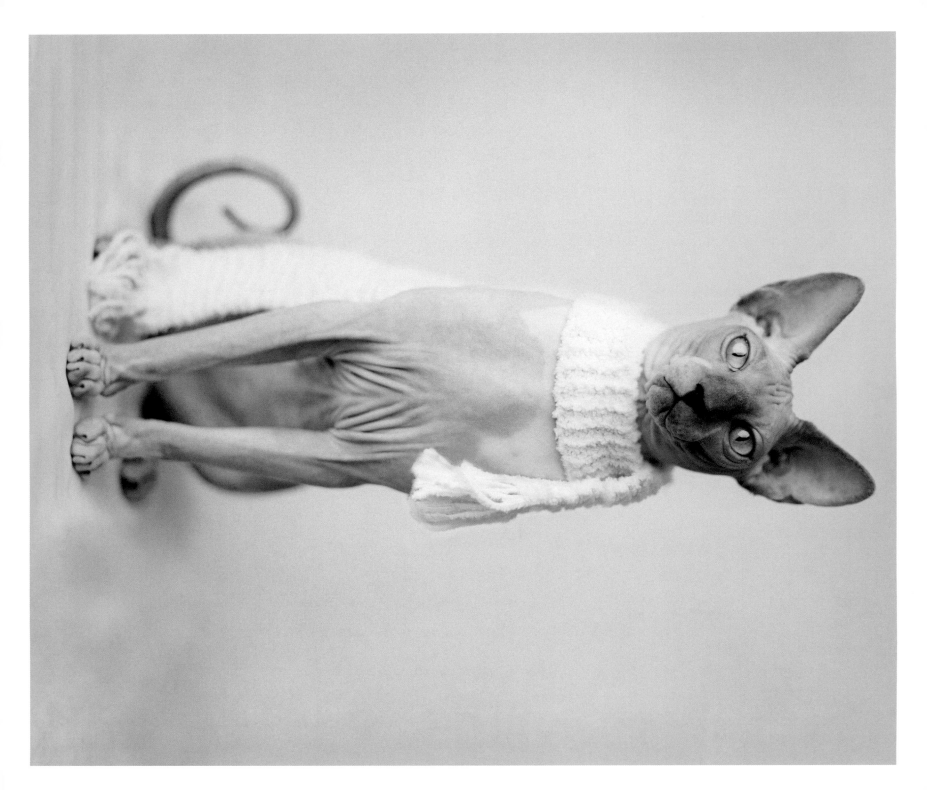

# HILANDER

▼ 79. SPHYNX

◀ 80. CHARLOTTE RED SELF PERSIAN

▲ 81. MR. SMEEGALL SEAL BURMESE

The owl and the pussy-cat went to sea,

In a beautiful pea-green boat;

They took some honey, and plenty of money,

Wrapped up in a five-pound note.

EDWARD LEAR

# HONEY

85. RAGDOLL CROSS ▼

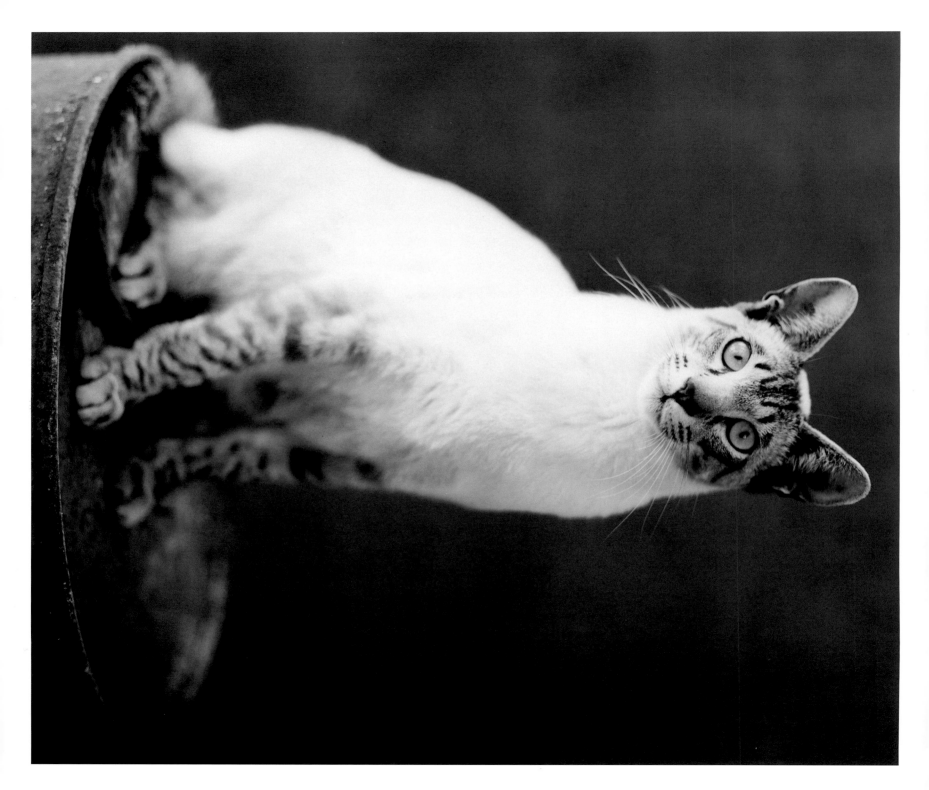

DIESEL

▼ 86. LYNX POINT SIAMESE

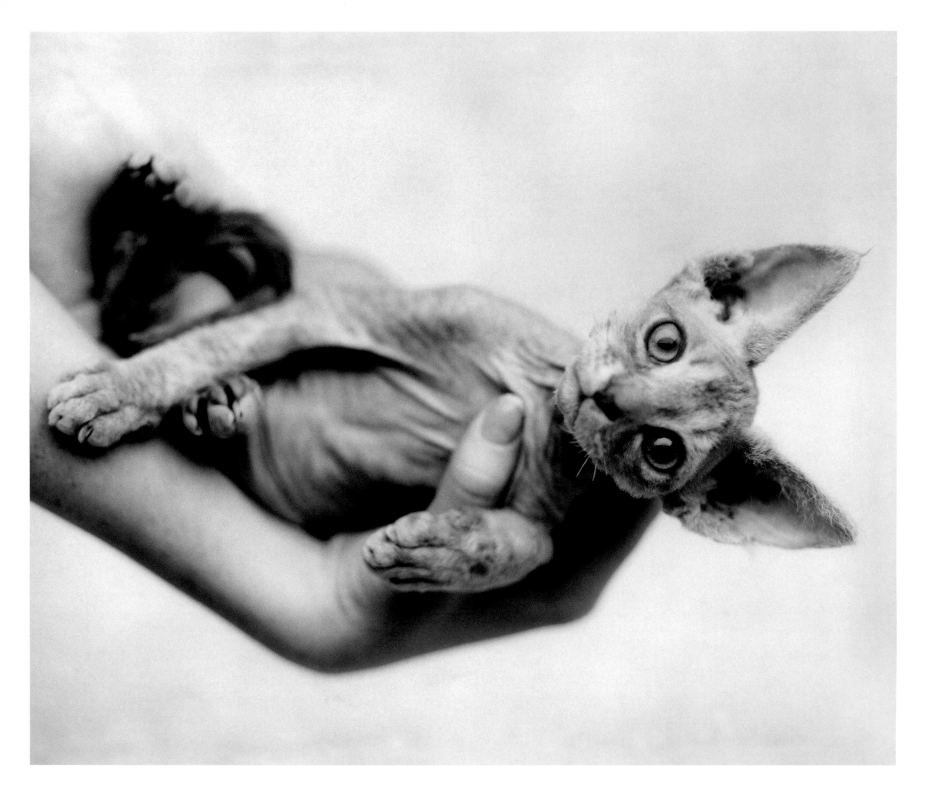

REX

Even a cat is a lion in her own lair.

**INDIAN PROVERB**

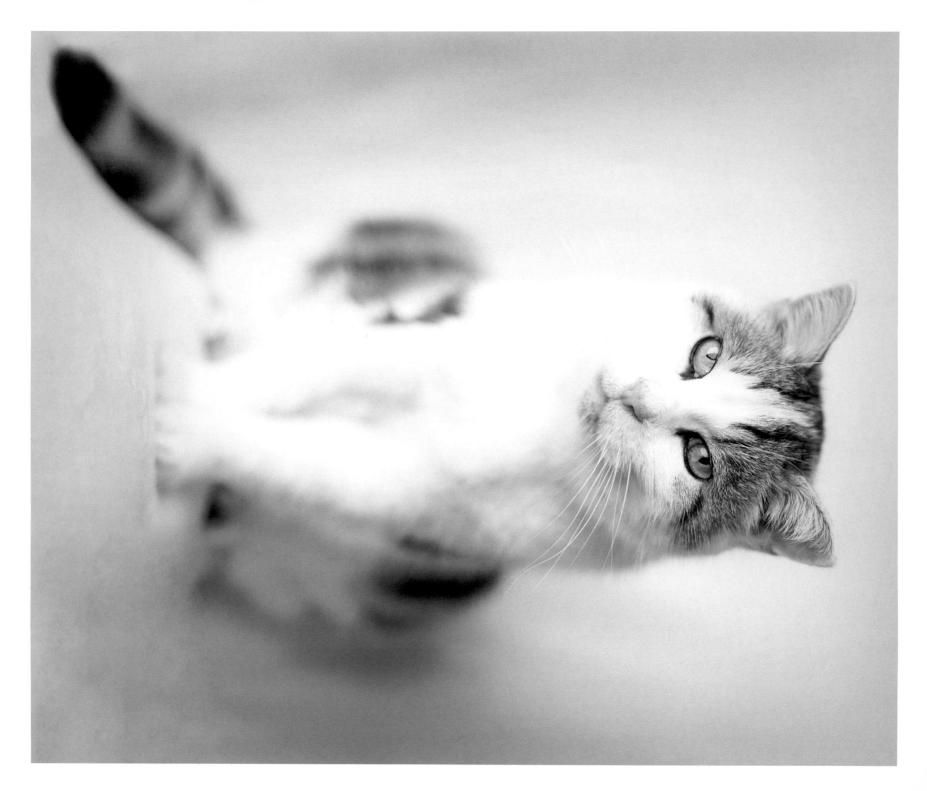

MCGUIVER
▼ 93. DOMESTIC SHORTHAIR

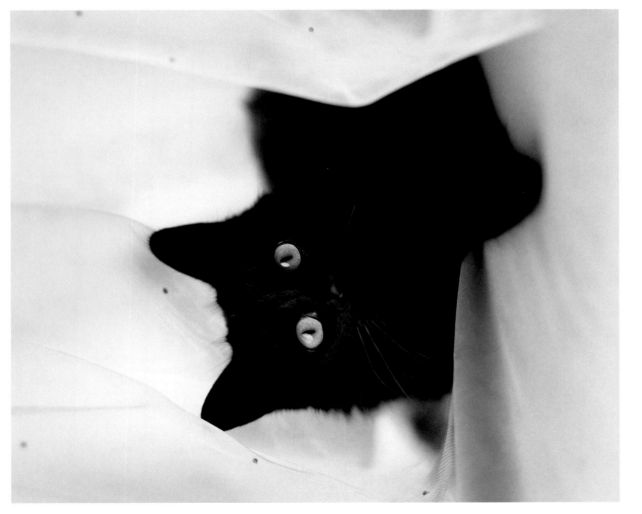

# REUBEN JAMES

96. FAWN POINT BALINESE ▼

CHARLIE & JOSIE OCICAT ▲▼ '97 & '98.

Thou art the Great Cat,

the avenger of the Gods

and the judge of words,

and the president of the sovereign chiefs

and the governor of the holy Circle;

thou art indeed...the Great Cat.

INSCRIPTION ON THE ROYAL TOMBS AT THEBES

99. STAR SILVER CLASSIC TABBY MAINE COON ▼

100 + 1

# APPENDIX

**1-4.**
**DOMESTIC SHORTHAIR**
**AND LONGHAIR**
**Hobbie, Mindy, Tyson, KC –**
**four weeks old**

It was a challenge to grab the attention of a gang of kittens intent on sliding down the smooth fabric. But perseverance and patience with animals always pays off – even if Tyson was caught off guard!

**5.**
**CHOCOLATE POINT PERSIAN**
**Sapphire – nine years old**

He may have played along, but Sapphire made it obvious he was not impressed at hanging in a sling. He would not offer a smile – just a catty smirk.

**6.**
**CHOCOLATE MANDALAY**
**Zoe – three months old**

Zoe was a cat acrobat, leaping through the air, scaling walls, trying to master the tightrope and snatch the feather toy as quick as a wink, so I had to be swift with the shutter to catch her the right way up.

**7.**
**BRITISH SHORTHAIR**
**Maximus – four weeks old**

He may have been barely four weeks old, but this little guy was born with a strong will – he was determined not to sit still on a human hand. After much wriggling, Maximus exhausted himself, and had no choice but to snuggle down and take a nap.

**8.**
**HIGHLAND VARIANT**
**Penelope – nine weeks old**

Like a graceful ballerina, Penelope turned pirouette after pirouette trying to catch a clutch of feathers, and paused for but a brief moment, mesmerized by her prey.

**9.**
**LILAC POINT BALINESE**
**Zen – seven weeks old**

Little Zen, shy and coy, was encouraged to take a peek from his hiding place with a little sweet-talking.

**10.**
**TEMPLE CAT**
**Wizard of Oz – eight weeks old**

Unlike Zen, Wizard of Oz was a jack-in-the-box, so we had to work fast! My assistant had to keep her hand over the hole to stop him from immediately leaping out.

**11 & 12.**
**ASIAN SHORTHAIR**
**Sebastian and Azzurro – 12 weeks old**

This pair enjoyed hanging around in matching stockings, being entertained by flying feathers. But it wasn't long before they figured how to wriggle out and capture them.

**13 & 14.**
**BROWN MARBLED BENGAL**
**Sunrise and Dawn – ten weeks old**

Bengal kittens are full of mischief and boundless energy, so the best way to keep this bouncy pair in hand was to swathe them together in soft fabric and suspend them gently off the ground.

**15.**
**BLUE POINT BRITISH SHORTHAIR**
**Yabba Dabba Doo – eight weeks old**

Yabba Dabba Doo was happy to be put in a pocket to be photographed – it turned out to be the perfect way to keep a rascally kitten still.

**16.**
**BIRMAN**
**Vivaldi – three weeks old**

It's not often you get to work with a tiny, fragile three-week-old kitten, and credit must be given to Vivaldi's breeder, who gently stroked him to sleep in the little box so we could capture this magical image of a sleeping beauty.

**17.**
**LYNX POINT RAGDOLL**
**Toby – eight weeks old**

Ragdolls – so floppy and flexible – were perfect cats for this image, and I had five of them taking turns dozing in the little hammock. It was Toby who stole the show with his classic Ragdoll flop.

**18 & 19.**
**DOMESTIC LONGHAIR**
**Gianni and Versace – one year old**

My own "designer moggies" – brothers and bundles of trouble. Just because their mum is the photographer doesn't mean they are born models. I captured just two images of the terrors before they dashed back into the garden.

**20.**
**WHITE ORIENTAL**
**Cupcake – 10 weeks old**

Despite an exhausting game of chase, Cupcake was determined not to fall asleep amongst the dessert. We had to fool her with a box placed over the dish before she fell into a deep slumber; unmoved by the aroma of fresh cupcakes.

21.
**LILAC BRITISH SHORTHAIR**
Barnaby – nine weeks old

After a morning frolicking with his kitten friends, Barnaby curled up to sleep in his soft, fleecy blanket. A little tickle under the chin in his catnap, and he fashioned a lazy smile.

22.
**PERSIAN**
Dreamy Lace – ten years old

This cat and I have a long and successful working relationship. Every time I photograph her, she closes her eyes. It isn't hard to capture an image of her sleeping – even though I know she is wide awake under those heavy lids!

23.
**BIRMAN**
Marc Anthony – eight weeks old

Who wouldn't fall asleep with a smile on their face, after being gently patted and placed on a soft bed of silk?

24 & 25.
**DOMESTIC SHORTHAIR**
Guiness and Fatboy – eight weeks old

It took a few hours of patient waiting while these cat brothers raced around. Finally there was no energy left and they collapsed in a contented sleep, curled together inside a bowl.

but little did her owners know she would grow up to be an explorer, roaming the neighborhood on her next adventure.

26.
**BIRMAN CROSS**
Saasha – 11 years old

This cat has style and a penchant for classy accessories – she puts up a mean fight to keep visitors' handbags and shoes. Saasha is also a real smoocher and loved basking in the sun on black velvet.

27.
**CYMRIC**
Ramsey – eight years old

Ramsey was not the least bit interested in me when we first met – she was far too busy stalking prey out in the bushes. But on her day before the camera, she was the model of tolerance and good manners.

28.
**TIFFANIE**
Danielle – three and a half years old

When I first met the magisterial Danielle, she was serving "time out" – sent to her room for bossing around the other cats in the household. When we met again, she was on her best behavior for the lens.

29.
**RUSSIAN BLUE CROSS**
Trinity – four years old

Mixed with the affection and intelligence of this cat is a hint of attitude. As I was leaning in to take this shot, Trinity reached out a paw as if we were communicating in our own special language.

30.
**RAGDOLL**
Angel – three months old

Angel was a perfect example of a Ragdoll – totally relaxed and floppy,

31.
**DOMESTIC TABBY**
Cougar – two years old

Swimming may be rare behavior for a cat, but Cougar eagerly dived into a tub of warm suds. His keenness was heightened by the promise of a treat, so he was oblivious to the bubbles bobbing around him.

32.
**HIMALAYAN PERSIAN**
Edmund – four and a half months old

Ed, my beloved crazy cat, is a gutter snipe – happy to nap in the drains along our street. Understandably, he needs bathing often – this was his first plunge at four months old.

33.
**CHOCOLATE PERSIAN**
Rascal – nine weeks old

This is one of my favorite photos. Knowing Rascal is always a rascal, it was no surprise he spent most of the time spinning around in the vase chasing his tail.

34.
**PERSIAN**
Baronosski – ten years old

Baronosski is a champion show cat, so taking a bath before showing his best side to the camera was second nature for him.

## 35.
### CHAMPAGNE BURMESE
**Chino – 18 months old**

Unlike most cats – especially the spirited Burmese – Chino was a little unsure of the drift of feathers circling his head, but his innate curiosity eventually got the better of him.

## 36.
### DOMESTIC SHORTHAIR
**Guiness – two years old**

Never let anyone say you can't pull the wool over a cat's eyes! Guiness is an incredibly tolerant cat who will wear his beanie at a jaunty angle – even if it means he cannot see a thing!

## 37 & 38.
### RUSSIAN BLUE
**Alexei and Cossak – eight weeks old**

Russian Blues are shy, quiet cats, and when Alexei and Cossak had their first experience out in the big, wide world, they became cat contortionists, timidly backing into the far reaches of the box.

## 39.
### DOMESTIC LONGHAIR
**Vincent – four years old**

Vincent wore an air of sophistication, complemented by his blue fur cap and stole. It was not difficult to persuade this gentleman to pose for the camera.

## 40.
### SCOTTISH FOLD
**Merlin – eight weeks old**

This busy little magician ran around the house for hours with his wizard cap on, refusing to come to a halt until sleep descended on him – fortunately with the hat still balanced on his head.

## 41.
### BROWN TABBY TIFFANIE
**Venezia – ten weeks old**

It was a difficult lesson learned when five kittens were introduced to the intoxication of crumpled newspaper. Venezia was the only one among them who sat still for the single minute needed to capture her portrait.

## 42.
### DOMESTIC SHORTHAIR
**Clayton – six months old**

It was a case of the country cat comes to the city, and Clayton, who lives in a farmyard barn, brought his best manners with him. The cat with the incredible eyes placed his paws exactly where asked – even inside the foreign territory of a city shopping bag.

## 43.
### DOMESTIC LONGHAIR
**Chloe – ten years old**

The Hansel and Gretel technique – food laid out in a strategic trail – was invented for Chloe, who performed perfectly once she realized there was a reward at the end of the box.

## 44.
### RED TABBY EXOTIC
**Teddy – two years old**

Teddy could have been straight out of the cartoon strip *Garfield* – what a character! Although we wanted him inside the roll of paper, he decided he wanted a reversal of roles, and got the camera in there instead.

## 45.
### ASIAN SHORTHAIR
**Toscano – six months old**

This is one hilarious, curious cat. If there was no sign of Toscano,

you only had to look in the film bag, or the light case…or in, under and over anything. It seemed perfectly natural to capture him discovering somewhere new.

## 46.
### SILVER TABBY EXOTIC
**Buster – three years old**

Buster, a cat infamous for stealing his neighbors' hairbrushes, wins the award for the longest shoot. He was happy to play with us all day, but it took him seven hours to get the gist of staring down the lens.

## 47.
### DOMESTIC SHORTHAIR
**Goku – six months old**

The sweetest-natured cat I have ever caught on film, Goku spent as much time cuddling and cavorting as he did getting down to business. He would cock his head like a dog when listening to directions.

## 48.
### DOMESTIC TABBY
**Winnie – three and a half years old**

Intrigued as I photographed his housemate Goku, Winnie demanded a taste of the limelight. This shot was captured between his attempts to whip off with the cream on freshly-baked scones in the kitchen.

## 49.
### SEAL LYNX ORIENTAL
**Jenny Any Dots – four months old**

This tiny little kitten – so fragile, yet so robust and full of energy – revelled in the chance to tangle with the usually forbidden basket of wool.

**50.**
**BROWN SPOTTED BENGAL**
Lu-lu – nine weeks old

Lu-lu is a sweet wee girl, but full of kittenish antics. She sat still just long enough for her bold Bengal spots not to become a blur.

**51.**
**ISLE OF MAN**
Big Boy Puss – three years old

The cat otherwise known as B.B. Puss was a border at a breeder I was visiting, and no one could ignore a face that exuded such charm and character.

**52.**
**ASIAN LEOPARD**
Naomi – 11 years old

Looks can deceive – Naomi has the face of a wildcat, but she is gentle and loving. She would stalk through the long grass towards the chicken coop, from where we would retrieve her so she could do it all over again.

**53.**
**LAVENDER MANDALAY**
Jenny Lavender – three years old

It required much persuasion to get Jenny Lavender to sit amongst her fragrant namesake flowers – the strong scent simply did not appeal to her. She even refused her favorite meal of liver, but was lured to the spot with tiny titbits of cheese.

**54.**
**EBONY ORIENTAL**
Black Elle – two years old

Strange as it may sound, Black Elle loves to pick a bouquet of flowers from the garden and carry them around in her mouth. Of course, she would not do this for the camera, but she was happy to pose surrounded by her treasured blooms.

**55.**
**CYMRIC**
Crosby – 12 years old

Crosby can proudly claim to be the only cat who gave me a war wound. With a swift swipe of claws across my wrist, establishing who was boss, he had no problem lying on the warm pebbles – like his favorite spot atop the concrete water tank at home.

**56.**
**SEAL BURMESE**
Errol – six years old

It's no wonder this cat goes by the name Feral Errol, drawing blood from his owner's cheek and leg during the shoot. But to show there were no hard feelings, the following morning Errol delivered a gift of wild rabbit to the foot of the bed.

**57.**
**MAINE COON**
Romeo – one year old

If I were a cat, I would have found my Romeo. Handsome, gentle and with a heart of gold, this Romeo was happy to do whatever was asked of him.

**58.**
**NORWEGIAN FOREST CAT**
Carl – two and a half years old

Thrilled by a new twig to tease, it took this forest cat some time before he stopped cavorting and posed in his own majestic style.

**59.**
**RUDDY ABYSSINIAN**
Tin Tin – six months old

Even though Abyssinians are celebrated hunters, Tin Tin was enthralled at being "captured" in a net, entertained by cat toys.

**60.**
**SNOW MARBLED BENGAL**
Castello – ten weeks old

This little guy would do anything for a tummy rub, and was happy to lie back on my assistant's lap and purr for the camera.

**61.**
**DEVON REX**
Kango – six years old

Kango is one cool cat who did not mind donning glasses – perhaps it even helped him focus on the morsels of meat dangled above the lens.

**62.**
**CREAM EUROPEAN BURMESE**
Ciaren – six years old

My "Mr. Cruise" lay anywhere but where I wanted him – on the book. He was eventually persuaded with the tactical placing of treats on the fold and a much appreciated rub under the chin.

**63.**
**DOMESTIC SHORTHAIR**
Scruffy – eight and a half weeks old

Scruffy is a tiny guy with an enormous personality. He was adopted from an animal welfare center and taken to a loving new home, where he caused chaos and destruction. I guess being so little means you can get away with a lot.

**64.**
**BRITISH SHORTHAIR**
Black Knight – 11 weeks old

Amongst a cute kindle of kittens, it was only Black Knight who boldly stepped forward to the lens. He was so laid back and cooperative, the perfect image was captured in a matter of minutes.

**65.**
**BURMILLA**
Jezita – three months old

Kittens can squeeze into the most remarkable spaces, like between the bars of a birdcage. Jezita was fooled by our feather teaser into thinking she had snared the prize.

**66.**
**LYNX BI-COLOR RAGDOLL**
Dexter – seven weeks old

From the word go, Dexter was the little troublemaker in his tribe – the youngest, smallest and naughtiest of five Ragdoll kittens. The moment his siblings snuggled down to sleep, Dexter would pounce.

**67 & 68.**
**DOMESTIC SHORTHAIR**
Samuel and Suzy – eight weeks old

These two mischievous cats were mesmerized by a feather on the end of a stick – before they discovered how to scramble out of the vase.

**69.**
**COLOR POINT TABBY RAGDOLL**
Willow – nine weeks old

Willow was content to lie totally relaxed on her pedestal bed, while we wrestled with the other kittens who were trying to snatch the cat toys we waved about to keep the subject awake.

**70.**
**MITTED TABBY RAGDOLL**
Misty – nine weeks old

It was a tight squeeze to get this little tabby Ragdoll inside the vase – she had grown so much in the two weeks since I first met her! It became all too obvious that my plan to get two kittens in there would never see the light of day.

**71.**
**CREAM POINT PERSIAN**
Puffy – six months old

It was love at first sight when I met Puffy, a debonair fellow with cheeks of blushed apricot. The challenge was to stop him hiding his natural good looks as he burrowed under the cozy blanket.

**72.**
**BLUE POINT BRITISH SHORTHAIR**
Casper – five weeks old

Three little bundles of fluff tried out for this image, but it was Casper who artfully draped a limb over the lip of the jug, while the others got lost inside.

**73.**
**SHADED SILVER PERSIAN**
Nevada – five years old

Nevada hails from the chilly climes of 46 degrees south and is used to the cold, but still loved snuggling into the warm fur tube.

**74.**
**SHADED SILVER PERSIAN**
Kaspar – six years old

Kaspar has the largest eyes I have ever seen on a cat, and he has huge paws, a big gentle nature and a mighty laid-back attitude to match. He lolled about, happy to be entertained.

**75.**
**DOMESTIC MEDIUM HAIR**
Charlie – two years old

The last cat to be photographed for the book, Charlie was adopted by my friends to soften the recent loss of their beloved Newfoundland dog, George. Charlie immediately took charge of his new home, bossing everyone around, including my 170-lb. Newfoundland, Henry.

**76.**
**TONKINESE**
Sara – four years old

Sara took a break from napping, nuzzled into the side of her closest buddy, a Rhodesian Ridgeback named Azizi, to pose nonchalantly for the camera.

**77.**
**KORAT**
Oscar – three years old

This was a one-shot wonder. Oscar, the stud cat, spent most of the time rubbing against everything in the room. Fortunately, in his quest for another new surface, he ventured under the mesh and peered out for just a split-second.

**78.**
**DOMESTIC SHORTHAIR**
**Pat the Cat – six years old**

Cool cat Pat is often found taking a ride in (or on top of) stranger's cars. But he's just as happy on stable ground as long as there's plenty of human attention – hence this shot with a pat on the head.

**79.**
**SPHYNX**
**Hilander – nine months old**

There is something fantastic about a hairless cat, but Hilander instantly won my heart. He may have felt a little strange to pat but like a genuine Sphynx, he was playful and fun.

**80.**
**RED SELF PERSIAN**
**Charlotte – eight years old**

A fluffy bundle of cuddles and cat kisses, Charlotte is the most affectionate feline I've ever met, with the cutest squeak of a meow that melts your heart.

**81.**
**SEAL BURMESE**
**Mr. Smeegall – seven months old**

Burmese are the most adventurous and gregarious cats and a great challenge to capture on film. To contain Mr. Smeegall's zeal, he was lured inside a cardboard box by a feather toy waggled in front of his nose.

**82.**
**BOMBAY**
**Tahlullah – seven and a half years old**

The slinky Tahlullah may be stone deaf, but she is not dumb. She could never be shut out while other cats were being photographed – with an uncanny ability to open doors then muscle her feline rivals out of the way.

**83.**
**ABYSSINIAN CROSS**
**Nikon (and Nigel) – 12 years old**

Nikon is a gentle giant of a cat who did not flicker a whisker with brave Nigel perched on his head (and the mouse even left his "calling card" there).

**84.**
**DOMESTIC TABBY**
**Cougar – two years old**

Cougar, the famous water-loving cat, was content to sit in a light shower, as long as he was protected by a doll's raincoat and hat.

**85.**
**RAGDOLL CROSS**
**Honey – two years old**

So as not to risk Honey being stung, we collected bees that had died naturally in their hive, and attached them to her coat using double-sided tape.

**86.**
**LYNX POINT SIAMESE**
**Diesel – ten months old**

One of most striking cats I have had the pleasure to photograph, Diesel was also a breeze to work with. He would pose, jump off his old tin drum, let out a classic Siamese yowl, then leap back up again for more.

**87.**
**CORNISH REX**
**Yoda – four months old**

Apparently, Yoda's daily "crazy time" ends at 11 a.m., but in front of the camera it took him a little longer to slow down to anything less than a blur.

His spirit made me fall in love with the Cornish Rex breed.

**88.**
**CORNISH REX**
**Bad Boy Bob – two years old**

The name suggests a wayward cat, yet Bad Boy Bob was long, lean, fast, cheeky and adorable – but never bad. All the same, he wasn't keen to hang around for long.

**89.**
**DEVON REX**
**Rex – ten weeks old**

Cradling Rex in tender hands was the perfect way to show off his remarkable soft and almost furless coat. He reminds me of E.T., my favorite movie character as a child.

**90.**
**EGYPTIAN MAU**
**Cairo – two and a half years old**

After lugging 30 concrete blocks up to a third floor apartment to create our set, we sat back and watched Cairo and her pal Rameses investigate their new playground. Before the lens, Cairo showed all the elegance and beauty of an Egyptian queen.

**91.**
**SOMALI**
**Monty – three years old**

Abyssinians are a real handful and the Somali (the long haired version), is just as active and demanding, but a little more laidback… or maybe that's just Monty, a perfect gentleman.

## 92.
### DOMESTIC MEDIUM HAIR
**Kirby – eight years old**

Kirby quivered by the cat door, then hid behind the couch, before being cajoled by two cat-mates – and a few little treats and comforting caresses – to join in the fun.

## 93.
### DOMESTIC SHORTHAIR
**McGuiver – 15 years old**

The oldest cat to grace this book, McGuiver felt his dignity was dented by having to pose for the camera. But the veteran could not hide a frivolous past – as a youth he thought he could fly by leaping out a second-story window.

## 94.
### CHOCOLATE SHADED BURMILLA
**Vadar – one year old**

The first session of this shoot had to be postponed when Vadar unexpectedly went out for a walk along one of the city's busiest streets. This urban feline takes everything in his stride, and when he was ready he was happy to pose in his owner's apartment.

## 95.
### JAVANESE
**Jessie – one year old**

Javanese cats are fearless with an insatiable curiosity and Jessie was in her element hanging off the curtains. She would have played for hours entangled in the mesh, had we not convinced her we had homes of our own to go to.

## 96.
### FAWN POINT BALINESE
**Reuben James – ten months old**

Reuben James simply claimed the box we had made for him. Although he barely moved a muscle, his soft coat was so thick and luxuriant there was fawn hair flying everywhere around the set!

## 97 & 98.
### OCICAT
**Charlie and Josie – one year old**

These intelligent but mischievous siblings had been taught to sit on command, but they were yet to learn to stay. It became a mission to stop Charlie bringing his favorite toy, a large wooden spoon, into the frame.

## 99.
### SILVER CLASSIC TABBY MAINE COON
**Star – five months old**

Star is a strong, serene and magnificent specimen who deserved her place on the pedestal. Maine Coons are large cats (myth has it they were bred from raccoons!), and our tiny Bengal kitten, Lu-lu, was just a quarter of Star's size, although not far apart in age.

## 100 & 101.
### BROWN SPOTTED TABBY BENGAL
**Basbouschka and Charisma – five weeks old**

I love the way cats curl up together in sleep. As if by instinct, Basbouschka and Charisma coiled themselves into the yin and yang position, and fell into a deep, blissful slumber.

ACKNOWLEDGMENTS

It has taken a team effort to produce 101 Cataclysms, and unfortunately it is impossible to mention and thank every individual, but I am extremely grateful to everyone who helped me turn this project into such an achievement.

Firstly, I would like to thank the two assistants I had while making this book: Nathalie Giacomelli and Charlotte Anderson. You both gave me endless patience and enthusiasm, two attributes that are absolute necessities when working with cats.

My business partners, David and Tanya Todd, also deserve special thanks for their invaluable support and encouragement over the years – allowing me to be as creative as I can be.

Thank you to the other members of our team in New Zealand, especially Robine Harris (design and retouching) and Sandra Seton, along with Richard Horton (UK and Europe) and Eric Kuskey (USA). You have all contributed so much – not only with our last two books, but with many other projects to date, and no doubt, in the future.

Once again, Geoff Blackwell and Ruth-Anna Hobday of PQ Publishers, have given me the freedom that all artists dream of – to be able to create images so close to my heart. Your dedication and support is invaluable and it is thanks to you that these images are shared with people around the world. To Jenny and Kylie, your effort with the production and design of 101 Cataclysms is greatly appreciated. Thank you to the rest of the team at PQ for being so wonderful to work with. Thanks also to Suzanne McFadden for helping me put into words my descriptions of the images.

This book would not have been possible without my good friends, Rae and John Field. Not only were they always there with a hot cup of tea after a long day's shoot, but they looked after my beloved Newfoundland, Henry, while I was out "capturing" cats. Sadly, Henry's best pal George, the Fields' Newfoundland, passed away near the completion of 101 Cataclysms. The hole in their lives was soon filled by the adoption of a cat called Charlie, who would become a star of this book. Unfortunately, the arrival of Charlie did not impress Henry, who simply wanted his old buddy back.

The team at Onewa Road Veterinary Clinic in Auckland, especially Richard Lucy who introduced me to so many wonderful cats.

I am also grateful to Image Centre (scanning), PCL (colour print processing), Labtec (black and white print processing) and Apix for their fast, efficient service in delivering my film, especially on the days I had left it to the last minute.

And of course an ENORMOUS thanks to all the cats and their owners for allowing me to capture the essence of these fabulous felines on film.

My final thanks goes to all my friends and family, who constantly support and encourage me, especially my parents, Bob and Barbara, and my twin sister, Rebecca, who are always thrilled to see new images and to offer an opinion. I love you all heaps, and again hope I have made you proud.

Bulfinch Press

Time Warner Book Group
1271 Avenue of the Americas, New York, NY 10020
Visit our Web site at www.bulfinchpress.com

First North American Edition
Published by arrangement with PQ Publishers Limited

Fifth Printing, 2005

ISBN 0-8212-6181-9

Library of Congress Control Number 2004107414

Designed by **Kylie Nicholls**

Text by **Suzanne McFadden**

Printed by **Everbest, China**